HARVEST OF A QUIET EYE

The Reverend Tim Heaton is an Anglican priest in parish ministry in the diocese of Salisbury. He is the author of *The Naturalist and the Christ* and *The Long Road to Heaven*, and a contributor to BRF's *New Daylight* Bible reading notes. He lives with his wife Arabella in north Dorset.

You can connect with him at facebook.com/lentcourses

"A skilful devotional writer" – *Church Times*

Harvest Of A Quiet Eye

Reflections in lockdown

Tim Heaton

Copyright © 2020 Tim Heaton

ISBN: 9798682744947

All rights reserved, including the right to reproduce this book, or portions thereof in any form. No part of this text may be reproduced, transmitted, downloaded, decompiled, reverse engineered, or stored, in any form or introduced into any information storage and retrieval system, in any form or by any means, whether electronic or mechanical without the express written permission of the author.

"Happiness is the harvest of a quiet eye"

Austin O'Malley

FOREWORD

It was an almost eerie experience not being able to worship in church for sixteen weeks. Of course we could *pray* at home, but that's not the same thing at all. Worship involves rites and ceremonies, beautiful liturgies, stirring hymns and, by no means least, the body broken and the blood outpoured. For me, Zoom services – as good as they were at filling a gap – largely failed to achieve any mystery, whilst streamed services, with the minister alone present in the church, seemed to lack spirit. Worship at its best is a communal activity because Christianity is about community.

So I began to hunger for a truer experience of worship and quickly discovered it not as I sat in front of my computer screen but in the cathedral of the great outdoors. I don't mean that I stood alone in the middle of a field singing *How Great Thou Art* at the top of my voice; rather I caught glimpses of the kingdom of heaven in the natural world all around me, and began to worship the Creator in the very theatre that God created. I know that to some extent I had always done that, but now I was doing it more easily and intensely than before.

Now I must be careful here. Whilst I am a great lover of nature and the proud owner of an 1861 edition of Reverend Gilbert White's *The Natural History of Selborne*, I'm not a particular devotee of natural theology. Natural theology, which came of age in the Victorian era, holds to the idea that the natural world acts as a window into the character and purposes of God, that the God who made the world can be known through the world that God created. It rests upon the assumption that the world is a benign and well-ordered realm, in which one can see the hand of a kind and gentle Creator. The hymn *All Things Bright and Beautiful*, written in 1848, conveys this idea: "How great is God Almighty, who has made all things well." The notion that nature was at heart benevolent had become one of the presumptions of the age.

Try telling that to someone being chased by a crocodile. The reality is that the natural world can also be cruel and violent, harsh and unforgiving. So whilst this little book has a distinct leaning towards observations of nature, as well as ecological and environmental issues, I am not an enthusiast of natural theology. (It is to Jesus we must look to know what God is really like.) My observations of nature simply became a springboard for worship – for adoration, awe and reverence, in wonder, love and praise – at a time when the church's doors were securely locked. In essence, I became more acutely aware of the place of humankind within the entire created order. I was mindful that something much bigger was still going on all around us as humanity fussed and fretted – quite rightly so in the face of a terrible death toll – over a particular coronavirus that had been given the name Covid-19.

Tim Heaton
Gillingham, Dorset
The Feast of Bartholomew, 2020

Day 1

Wednesday, 18 March

Today I watched the tadpoles, thousands of them, starting to wriggle out of their jelly in our pond. And Jesus said, "Take heart, it is I; do not be afraid."

Day 2

Thursday, 19 March

Amongst the primroses and the common dog violets in our wildflower garden, a clump of red dead-nettle has flowered today. Yellow, red and blue together, the primary colours of God's palette. And Jesus said, "Do not let your hearts be troubled. Believe in God, believe also in me."

Day 3

Friday, 20 March

This morning at breakfast I watched a song thrush cracking open a snail against a stone. (The ramsons - wild garlic - are already up by the pond, and I wondered whether she'd like some of that with her snails.) And Jesus said, "Look at the birds of the air; they neither sow nor reap nor gather into barns, and yet your heavenly Father feeds them."

Day 4

Saturday, 21 March

This afternoon I solemnized the marriage of Sarah and James (love is all around) in the beautiful church that overlooks the famous National Trust gardens at Stourhead. The church has stood for more than 700 years as a silent witness to other plagues. Stourhead is now closed for the duration, the church is not. And Jesus said, "Remember, I am with you always, to the end of the age."

Day 5

Sunday, 22 March – Mothering Sunday

This morning I went to the church in Milton on Stour to pray. I gave thanks to God for our Blessed Mother Mary, for the Church, for your mother and mine, and for all who have been like mothers to us. And Jesus said, "Here are my mother and my brothers! For whoever does the will of my Father in heaven is my brother and sister and mother."

Day 6

Monday, 23 March

The sun is shining brightly in north Dorset, God is in his heaven, and the wallflowers are in full bloom. Known in the Middle Ages as the *chevisaunce*, an old word meaning comfort, the wallflower's heady scent was said to ward off bubonic plague. "Comfort, O comfort my people," says your God.

Day 7

Tuesday, 24 March

We haven't been able to buy loo paper for two weeks now. None in Waitrose yesterday and none in Morrisons today. It gives a whole new meaning to "going paperless"! But is this simply, as they call it, a first world problem? Have they ever had enough in all the refugee camps that have proliferated to the world's shame, and which are currently much more vulnerable to this virus than we'll ever be?

Day 8

Wednesday, 25 March – The Feast of the Annunciation

When the angel Gabriel appeared to Mary she was afraid. He said, "Fear not." Fear is the key that keeps us behind locked doors. Fear of other people. Fear of every fellow child of God who is now perceived to be a danger. Stay in if you can, but heed today the words of the angel: "Do not be afraid."

Day 9

Thursday, 26 March

I hope you've got a garden to enjoy, however small. The broad beans I sowed on 1st March, St David's Day, are already six inches tall, and yesterday, Lady Day, I sowed the first row of salad leaves – cut and come again. But if you haven't, I hope you can at least glimpse from a window God's garden, which is all around us. "My Father is the gardener," said Jesus, and God is still at work in his world.

Day 10

Friday, 27 March

There's a green lining to this quarantine: a cut in carbon emissions. Aeroplanes are grounded and cruise ships docked. Home working and online shopping are likely to become future norms for many more people. Can you dare to believe today that the way we had come to live our lives *needed* to be disrupted? And that something good might actually come from all of this once all the tears have dried?

Day 11

Saturday, 28 March

It's only just struck me that this quarantine – from the Italian word *quarantina* meaning forty days – has come during the forty days of Lent. I can only imagine that for many people, especially those who have never previously been observant of Lent, this has been a time of fasting and self-examination like never before. And penitence. "Holy God, holy and strong, holy and immortal, have mercy upon us."

Day 12

Sunday, 29 March – Passion Sunday

Lazarus was ill and he died. Jesus wept. It seems an appropriate gospel for today as the death toll mounts and the sounds of mourning are heard around the world. Lent gathers pace from today and the mood darkens, as we begin to anticipate Jesus's own suffering and death. But for now he's still with us. And he weeps.

Day 13

Monday, 30 March

I've just done my weekly Pilates class via You Tube. Tomorrow a staff meeting on Zoom. It's helpful, I know, but I don't think it's healthy. Tech experts are already saying the internet will get overwhelmed. Bandwidth will have to be rationed or restricted to essential services only. My daily prayer is already a litany of hopes for a return to the way things were. Lord, have mercy. Christ, have mercy. Lord, have mercy.

Day 14

Tuesday, 31 March

Oh dear, the Wine Society has stopped home deliveries! It says it can no longer ensure the safety of its employees. I applaud the motive but am left wondering what would happen if every other home delivery company decided to follow suit. Well, I've got to have my Jesus juice. I'll get it from the supermarket now. You see, I've always heeded St Paul's advice: "Take a little wine for the sake of your stomach and your frequent ailments."

Day 15

Wednesday, 1 April

The house has never been so clean. It's thanks to Arabella, of course, but a sure sign of our confinement. We're pacing up and down like caged animals, only there's no one outside looking at us through the bars. This restriction of liberties already feels like incarceration. And there are no clocks in prison, only calendars. Lord Jesus, set the captives free.

Day 16

Thursday, 2 April

News of the death of another medic hits hard, and it's right to applaud all who are working in the front line of this pandemic. It was once fallen soldiers who were likened to crucified Christs, but now "the Christ who dies for our sins is the health worker" (Simon Kuper, FT). It's a stirring thought as we draw nearer to Holy Week and the greatest story of self-sacrifice ever told.

Day 17

Friday, 3 April

Three impossibilities for Europe's refugees:
1. Stay at home.
2. Wash hands with soap and hot water.
3. Maintain social distancing.
It's a terribly unfair world. Let's not forget them. Today I'm counting my blessings and I hope that you can count some too.

Day 18

Saturday, 4 April

The hedgerows are daubed with splodges of white: The blackthorn blossom is out. A sure sign of Easter hope and joy, keeping the promise alive. But its spikes are sharp and sturdy, over one inch long, and once they made a crown of thorns. It isn't Easter yet. There are seven days starting tomorrow we have to get through first. Sorry, but there is no Easter Day without Good Friday.

Day 19

Sunday, 5 April – Palm Sunday

Heat. Dust. Cloaks. Branches. Turmoil. "Look, your king is coming to you, humble, and mounted on a donkey." A police car arrives to break up the crowds. "Go home!" a policeman shouts. "You've all been told to stay at home!"

But still they sing: Hosanna to the Son of David! Hosanna to the King of kings!

Day 20

Monday, 6 April – Holy Monday

Smell the fragrance of the costly perfume that filled the house of Martha and Mary and Lazarus-who-once-was-dead. Sense its opulence and its luxury, its extravagance and its excess. Savour its wealth and its richness, its affluence and its indulgence. Now know the abundant love and devotion of Mary who poured it out, and pray that the same might overflow from you today.

Day 21

Tuesday, 7 April – Holy Tuesday

The row of mixed salad leaves I sowed on Lady Day germinated at the weekend once the warmer weather arrived. The seeds had lain buried in the ground for ten days, dead to the world, before the miracle of life after death began. And today Jesus says, "Very truly, I tell you, unless a grain of wheat falls into the earth and dies, it remains just a single grain; but if it dies, it bears much fruit."

Day 22

Wednesday, 8 April – Holy Wednesday

It's a full moon tonight, the first full moon of spring, the Passover moon, and it signals the start of the Jewish Passover, which begins at sundown. There was another Passover two millennia ago, when a man was betrayed by his friend. The same moon shone down that night, the very moon that the man who was betrayed had set in the dome of the sky.

Day 23

Thursday, 9 April – Maundy Thursday
(From the French *mandé* meaning "commandment")

All of human suffering is shared by God tonight: betrayal and brokenness; anguish and agony; desertion and denial; hatred and humiliation. But one thing pierces through it all, resounds in our hearts, and will conquer in the end: The new commandment, "Love one another as I have loved you."

Day 24

Friday, 10 April – Good Friday

Jesus died alone, save for another condemned man on either side of him. Kept back by the soldiers, those who loved him could only watch from a distance. My thoughts and prayers today are for all who have died and will die from Covid-19 alone, in hospitals and care homes, without their loved ones by their side. But still the promise remains: "Truly I tell you, today you will be with me in Paradise."

Day 25

Saturday, 11 April – Easter Eve

When Joseph of Arimathea got home last night and told his wife what he'd done, she went mad. "What! You mean you've given our own family tomb to that trouble-making blasphemer? We won't be able to use it ourselves now, it's contaminated – unclean!" "Don't worry, my love," Joseph replied, "he's only borrowing it for the weekend."

Day 26

Sunday, 12 April – Easter Day

https://youtu.be/jHffYxyevV0

Day 27

Monday, 13 April – Easter Monday

It was the strangest Easter Day ever. Five minutes spent recording a video and nine hours trying to upload it! I'm sorry you got it so late, but the internet was at breaking point all day and our broadband the speed of a snail. The video certainly won't win any Oscars, but at least it might count as a public proclamation of our Lord's great and glorious resurrection across our great and glorious benefice. The real sadness, of course, is that you weren't able to receive the Blessed Sacrament yourself – on Easter Day of all days. But together we can go on saying, Alleluia. Christ is risen. He is risen indeed. Alleluia.

Day 28

Tuesday, 14 April – Easter Tuesday

I saw an Orange-tip butterfly this morning flying over some Garlic mustard (a.k.a. Jack-by-the-hedge), which is one of the principal food sources of its caterpillar. This is the stuff that Easter is made of. Not just life, but life after death. Every cowslip and every bluebell is a resurrection, part of the passage from winter into spring, but one that chiefly signposts the Resurrection of our Lord and Saviour Jesus Christ. "Death has been swallowed up in victory. Where, O death, is your victory? Where, O death, is your sting?"

Day 29

Wednesday, 15 April – Easter Wednesday

There is Love behind the splendour of the spring,
when the weary winter dies and the Lord with laughing eyes
bids the trembling world arise, whispering:
"Did you think that God was dead?
No, my blood is warm and red,
and there is no death to dread, come and sing."

The Revd G A Studdert Kennedy, MC (1883 – 1929)

Day 30

Thursday, 16 April – Easter Thursday

I imagine the natural world is rather enjoying this human quarantine: far fewer interventions by homo sapiens (or homo not-so-sapiens as I often think of us). Lower air pollution and litter pollution from fewer car journeys is an obvious benefit, something that may become the new norm. Easter reminds us that there will be new life the other side of this. We mustn't lose sight of that. It may be a better life. "For God, all things are possible."

Day 31

Friday, 17 April – Easter Friday

I took my first lockdown funeral yesterday, that of a lovely man named Michael. I find that every funeral in Eastertide takes on a special quality because of the freshness and vitality of the Easter message concerning our new life in Christ. At this time, when all humanity is threatened by a tiny agent of death, we inevitably and quite naturally seek deliverance from this virus and from our fear of the end. But may we also go on celebrating our deliverance from death!

Day 32

Saturday, 18 April – Easter Saturday

This threat that brings us together in human solidarity also divides us, because lockdown exacerbates the inequalities between old and young, rich and poor. The old, though more at risk, are generally richer, so they can endure isolation in far greater comfort than the young who, though less at risk, are generally poorer. The young, deprived of the ability to earn their daily bread, are making sacrifices for the old. Because we know there is life the other side of this, we must seek a resurrection into better lives for all.

Day 33

Sunday, 19 April – Second Sunday of Easter
(Easter Day in the Orthodox Eastern Church)

In recent weeks we've all had to rethink every aspect of our church's life and ministry. We've had to do things differently – virtually and remotely. These creative and innovative responses have had impact: we're probably in contact with more people than before, and more often. But none of these things can ever replace the warmth of real human contact. In today's gospel, Jesus stands among his disciples. He speaks, he shows them his wounds and breathes the Holy Spirit on them. Actions performed "in the flesh". We will go back to it, but we'll also have learnt a great deal along the way.

Day 34

Monday, 20 April

Friday's rain has brought new life to the garden and one of my favourite wildflowers is blooming today – the yellow archangel. I wish I knew how it got its name. In

Christian tradition there are three archangels, who are also saints: Gabriel, bearer of the message to Mary; Michael, leader of the celestial armies and guardian of souls; and Raphael, chief of the guardian angels. If I had to guess I'd go for Gabriel, as the shape of the flower looks rather like the monogram of Maria that appears on the symbol of St Gabriel. Anyway, it's a great name for a wayside flower – much better than yellow archbishop or yellow archdeacon!

Day 35

Tuesday, 21 April

One of the great sadnesses of this lockdown is that our churches are… well, locked! The suspension of public worship and other gatherings of the faithful is one thing, but to allow no one to enter a church alone to pray seems harsh in these times when a renewed thirst for spiritual refreshment is evident. St Nicholas' Church in Silton was previously never locked, which was a wonderful thing, and I'm told the churchwardens had a job finding the key! Still, at least we know Jesus isn't locked in. For the risen Christ, no door is locked, no entrance barred.

Day 36

Wednesday, 22 April

When we emerge into our new life the other side of this, society should be the better for it. More people are reaching out to isolated neighbours, checking on the elderly, asking if they need food or medicines. Volunteering is on the up, not only amongst those who temporarily have no work but also those who previously had too much leisure time. Volunteering is a way of converting leisure into community, and there's no reason to think this won't continue. We've all become a little more human (made in God's image) and humane. We are more Christ-like, and the kingdom of heaven has come nearer.

Day 37

Thursday, 23 April – St George

St George never slayed a dragon, that was St Michael (Revelation 12:7-9), but somehow the exploits of Michael got absorbed into the legend of George. George was a Roman soldier martyred in Palestine in AD 303 for refusing to take part in the persecution of Christians. His story inspired the English armies during the Crusades to the Holy Land, and they adopted his symbol (the martyr's red cross) as their emblem. We might wish for a dragon-slayer today to vanquish this monstrous virus, but that's just fantasy. Instead we have a man who accomplished the greatest act of love. And love is always the victor because that is the power of God.

Day 38

Friday, 24 April

There's no doubt that going to church is a risky business. We sit close together, hold books that other people have held, drink from the same cup, shake hands a lot, and so on. If social distancing rules are, as we hear, going to remain in place for a considerable time, I wonder if this means we won't be going back to church for a long while. Is it really possible to be church in the conventional way and observe social distancing? But when we do, the upside is we'll have much more awareness of not passing on ordinary colds and flu. We know how to do it now: not coughing into the hand, more handwashing, and self-isolation for infectious people. And that will be another good that comes from all of this.

Day 39

Saturday, 25 April – St Mark the Evangelist

The Feast of St Mark always falls during Eastertide, the fifty days from Easter to Pentecost. I find that somewhat paradoxical as Mark's gospel itself tells us absolutely nothing about those days. Mark's gospel proper – ignoring the two endings which were later additions not written by Mark – ends at the empty tomb. No encounters with the risen Jesus. No Emmaus Road. No Doubting Thomas. No fishing on the lake. No Ascension. Nothing at all. Mark's gospel ends on the morning of the first Easter Day. And that's the thing about Easter for Mark: the tomb was empty. It's beautifully simple, and you either believe it or you don't.

Day 40

Sunday, 26 April – Third Sunday of Easter

In today's gospel, two disciples returning home to Emmaus after Passover in Jerusalem are joined by a stranger, who they only recognize later in the breaking of the bread.

Who is the third who walks always beside you?
When I count, there are only you and I together
But when I look ahead up the white road
There is always another one walking beside you
Gliding wrapt in a brown mantle, hooded
I do not know whether a man or a woman
– But who is that on the other side of you?

T S Eliot, *The Waste Land*

Day 41

Monday, 27 April

Yesterday morning I watched Sunday Worship on BBC1 from Hereford Cathedral. The hymns were from an old recording of Songs of Praise and included Charles Wesley's fabulous "And Can It Be", sung to the rousing tune *Sagina*. It made me realize how much I miss singing good hymns. (Not bad hymns, only good hymns!) It's such a big part of what makes churchgoing a communal activity, and one that simply can't be replicated in virtual form. Social networks and video apps are doing a great job today creating online communities, but it's doubtful they'll sustain their current appeal after lockdown is lifted. In so many ways it just doesn't compare to real life.

Day 42

Tuesday, 28 April

Exactly eight hundred years ago today, on 28th April 1220, the foundation stones of Salisbury Cathedral were laid. A commemorative art exhibition can now only be seen online, but many will enjoy this virtual tour: https://www.salisburycathedral.org.uk/spirit-and-endeavour-virtual-art-tour
Jacqueline Creswell, the Cathedral's Visual Arts Adviser and Curator says, "The exhibition was conceived as a celebration of the human spirit and human endeavour, manifested through the faith and skill that drove the Cathedral builders and their community on. That shared humanity and capacity to create and endure holds today and I hope this exhibition encourages viewers to look forward with hope." Amen to that.

Day 43

Wednesday, 29 April

I'm sure that all farmers, growers and gardeners will be appreciating this rain. The Holy Spirit abounds in my garden at the moment in the form of Columbine (Aquilegia), which gets its name from *columba*, the Latin word for "dove". The hanging flower looks just like a cluster of doves facing in on each other, and so the Columbine came to represent the Holy Spirit in Christian symbolism. Take a look, I bet you've got Columbine in your garden too. It's one of my favourite British native flowers, though I've never seen it growing in the wild in its natural form, always blue-violet, whereas garden varieties are often red, pink or white.

Day 44

Thursday, 30 April

Alleluia, Praise the Lord! Yesterday, for the first time since early March, we've been able to buy wholemeal strong bread flour in the supermarket. We reached a crisis point a few weeks ago when it seemed that Arabella, for the first time ever, would not be able to bake our daily bread. But we managed then to get an emergency supply from an excellent loose goods emporium run by a certain Eve Pegler. Thank you Eve, like manna from heaven. But now it's back on the supermarket shelves and the baking goes on. Happiness. The harvest of a quiet eye.

Day 45

Friday, 1 May – St Philip and St James, Apostles

The James we commemorate today is the "lesser" James, son of Alpheus, rather than the "greater" James, son of Zebedee and brother of John. Apart from being named in the lists of the Twelve he isn't otherwise mentioned at all. Philip is (unfortunately for him) best remembered for failing to suggest how Jesus might feed the five thousand (John 6:5-7). He should have known what to say; after all,

Jesus had already turned water into wine. His unfortunate slip-up is for ever recorded in his symbol – two loaves of bread, one either side of a gold cross. Poor Philip, it seems like rubbing it in a bit! But even Satan knew that Jesus could turn stones into bread.

Day 46

Saturday, 2 May

To stretch the bread motif into a third day, yeast was also impossible to find on the supermarket shelves for many weeks, but supplies now seem to be back to normal. In Chaucer's time yeast was known as *godisgoode*, "bicause it cometh of the grete grace of God," though this might have had more to do with the fact that it was needed for making beer rather than bread! And it was Martin Luther who famously said, "Whoever drinks beer, he is quick to sleep; whoever sleeps long, does not sin; whoever does not sin, enters Heaven! Thus, let us drink beer!" Yes, God is good, and perhaps we should say it more often.

Day 47

Sunday, 3 May – Fourth Sunday of Easter

"I am the gate" (John 10:9). The image is of a sheepfold, a common sight in the Lake District (will we be able to go this summer?), an enclosure of rough stone walls with a single opening. It serves as a windbreak on the barren fells, providing shelter in severe weather. The sheep can come in and go out; there is no gate. The good shepherd becomes the gate. He lies across the opening to keep out the wolf. And he says to the sheep, "You see? You're completely safe now. Because there's only one way the wolf will be able to get in here, and that's over my dead body."

Day 48

Monday, 4 May

I can see light at the end of the tunnel. Life appears to be returning – slowly – to a semblance of normality, though I don't think we'll be completely back to normal for a considerable time yet. Last week I discovered that Sydenhams had reopened and I was able to pick up some DIY supplies. I was able to take my lawnmower in for repair. This week an electrician is coming to carry out some non-essential work. My mood has improved. Signs of hope. From the fig tree learn its lesson.

Day 49

Tuesday, 5 May

Traffic volumes have picked up a bit recently – I've been part of that as I admitted yesterday! – but I read that at the height of the lockdown there was 70 per cent less traffic on the roads. There's also 70 per cent less litter on the main road through Bourton. There are just fewer people making car journeys, eating and drinking on the move, and chucking the rubbish out the window! I pray that people won't go back to doing that. I hope they'll realize that "grab and go" is a sure way to catch a virus, but also that littering is a desolating sacrilege of God's good and beautiful creation.

Day 50

Wednesday, 6 May

Some of you have been telling me about the wildlife in your garden, thank you, and quite rightly rejoicing in it. But a woman here in Bourton told me the other day she's got adders. Yes, adders in Bourton! She only has a small garden, dogs, and naturally regards them with fear. I do feel sorry for her, but I also feel a bit sorry for the adders, beautiful creatures, a protected species, yet generally regarded with hostility. If you believe the story it's all Eve's fault (the first Eve not ours!), for falling for the crafty serpent's trick. "I will put enmity between you and the woman, and between your offspring and hers…" Still, their presence here is great news for naturalists and conservationists.

Day 51

Thursday, 7 May

I have a passion for wildflowers, plants as God created them, not modified by plant breeders for greater stature, vigour, colour or scent. I also have a sneaky suspicion that our native bees, bugs and butterflies prefer them. I planted some Corn cockle seedlings in our wildflower garden yesterday, which a friend had grown from seed. It's a rare plant today, almost extinct in the wild, but one that was once a common sight in Britain's wheat fields. A red-flowered "weed". I don't know if it will establish itself or not, but it's worth a try. It's just a little way of caring for God's creation, which usually needs a helping hand from us where we have contributed to its destruction.

Day 52

Friday, 8 May – VE Day 75

It's a terrible shame that so many community events have had to be cancelled today – on a bank holiday that was created especially for them. But we're still on a war footing. Nevertheless, we can still celebrate inwardly today, even if we can't do it too outwardly. There is indeed much to commemorate and to honour, and we should do just that. Christians, of all people, know how to rejoice. It's our tradition, it's in our DNA. We are Easter people and Alleluia is our song. So today we'll have a joyful heart.

Day 53

Saturday, 9 May

"On VE Day victory bells were rung at intervals throughout the day and the town presented an animated scene, the gaily decorated streets being filled with happy townspeople. The Gillingham Silver Prize Band played selections at Mill Road." (A report from 1945, reproduced in this month's issue of *The Gillingham Historian*.) How interesting to read about the day itself. I imagine it's just how the town would have been yesterday had all the planned events been able to go ahead. And what about today, seventy-five years ago? Rather a lot of sore heads, I'm sure, and perhaps some time for quieter reflection on the enormity of it all. "You shall go out with joy and be led forth in peace" (Isaiah 55:12).

Day 54

Sunday, 10 May – Fifth Sunday of Easter

"On Sunday, a united service of thanksgiving was held at St Mary's, to which the Home Guard, Royal Observer Corps, V.A.D., Civil Defence and other organisations had been invited. The church was filled as perhaps it has not been for years." (A report from 1945, reproduced in this month's issue of *The Gillingham Historian*.) The Sunday after VE Day was observed throughout the country as Thanksgiving Sunday. Time at last to give thanks to God for a "great deliverance". Today I went on my own to Milton church to pray. Open again, to clergy only at this time, but open nonetheless. Another sign of hope, and something else to give thanks for today.

Day 55

Monday, 11 May

All over the countryside the hawthorn blossom sits like snow on its boughs. The May Tree, symbol of new life, fertility and rebirth, whose blossoming branches ("may") were woven into May Day crowns. I'm sure I've read somewhere – though I can't find it now – that the hawthorn hosts more species of insect than any other of our native trees. It really is the bugs' best friend. So if you're thinking of planting a tree, just one tree, maybe it should be a hawthorn. We're lucky enough to have one in our back garden, the veg patch, where I reckon it helps maintain the population of ladybirds and other beneficial insects that feed on aphids and plant lice, getting the balance of nature right. Anyway, enjoy the may.

Day 56

Tuesday, 12 May

It was exactly eight weeks ago that public worship was suspended. And now the government's new roadmap for a phased recovery puts places of worship into Step 3, alongside hairdressers, pubs and cinemas, reopening "no earlier than 4 July". That's another eight weeks away, so it's going to be a long haul. But I'm glad they've ditched the "Stay Home" slogan, at least in England. Not because I want to go out but because it always infuriated me that the preposition *at* was missing! For now, Stay Alert. That's something we're good at… "for the Son of Man is coming at an unexpected hour."

Day 57

Wednesday, 13 May

I'm pleased that some garden centres have reopened today, and I expect you are too. Judging by the responses I get, my rambling thoughts you seem to like the most are about nature – the garden, countryside and wildlife. Some of you have also been submitting photos to the church website. Last weekend a beautiful photo appeared of Yellow Irises (Yellow Flags) growing by the Shreen. Quite gorgeous. Many flowers have a place in Christian tradition. The Iris is known as the "Sword Lily", on account of its long sword-shaped leaves, and portrays the sorrow of Mary for the Passion of Christ. "A sword will pierce your own soul too" (Luke 2:35).

Day 58

Thursday, 14 May – St Matthias, Apostle

Matthias was a follower of Jesus from the beginning, perhaps one of the Seventy, who after the Ascension was chosen by lot – a way of revealing who God had already chosen – to replace Judas Iscariot and bring the apostolate back to twelve. Empowered by the outpouring of the Holy Spirit at Pentecost, he served as a missionary in Judea until his martyrdom by stoning and beheading. In his window in Milton on Stour church, where the Twelve are all so beautifully portrayed in stained glass, he can be seen holding a large battle-axe, the instrument of his death and his symbol for all eternity.

Day 59

Friday, 15 May

The biggest thing coronavirus has shown is that a complete revolution in human behaviour is possible – and that it can happen very quickly. Why is it, then, that we can't seem to tackle other issues that so desperately need to be dealt with? The will of government is, of course, key. If it can force me to go for two months without a haircut, then surely it can better tackle drugs, crime (the one feeds the other), mental health, poverty, homelessness, pollution and climate change. It can't just be that coronavirus is a matter of life and death, because all these other things are too, some on an even bigger scale. Where there's a will there's a way. Pray for our leaders today.

Day 60

Saturday, 16 May

When I mentioned the prohibition on going to the hairdresser for two months, I actually meant four. It's been two months already and most likely it'll be another two. I'll look like Samson by the end of this. I know what you're thinking – Arabella can cut it! I think not, she's no more qualified for that than Delilah. I'll just let it grow. I had long hair in the 1970s; I might even go back to wearing flared trousers and platform boots as well. It'll be like *Life on Mars* (let the reader understand), travelling back in time to the seventies. And when this nightmare is finally all over, we'll realize just how brilliant it really is to be living on Earth.

Day 61

Sunday, 17 May – Sixth Sunday of Easter

As I sat in a cool and peaceful Silton church this morning and read today's Bible readings these words from Acts jumped out: "God does not live in temples made by human hands." And then the gospel affirmed it: Jesus said, "I am in you." You knew that already but isn't it brilliant? *I am in you.* It's great that our churches are being prayed in again but God does not live there. He lives in you and me, so that "by his continual presence in us he may raise us to eternal joy" (today's Collect, gathering everything up very nicely as always). The only thing living in Silton church right now is the vestry mouse. Efforts are continuing to trap her humanely and release her elsewhere. I'll keep you posted.

Day 62

Monday, 18 May

These three days before Ascension Day are the Rogation Days, when we ask for God's blessing on the land and for the protection of crops. In the Prayer Book tradition, yesterday was observed as Rogation Sunday. The BCP gospel begins, "Verily, verily I say unto you, Whatsoever ye shall ask the Father in my name, he will give it you" (John 16:23). So perhaps, over these three days, we can all say some prayers of petition and thanksgiving for the resources of the earth and for those who grow and produce our food. And remember: "In the world ye shall have tribulation; but be of good cheer, I have overcome the world" (John 16:33).

Day 63

Tuesday, 19 May

Someone emailed me immediately and said, "We should pray for rain." And she's right, we should. So far as I recall we've only had two spells of rain in the last couple of months, though the last time we did have quite a lot. But I've had the sprinkler on the vegetable garden already, much earlier than usual. So on this second Rogation Day I'm giving thanks to God for our plentiful supply of water. In the twenty-five years I've lived here we've never had a hosepipe ban. And I'm praying for those in other parts of the world who have not nearly enough, some even without clean water to drink, let alone water to irrigate their crops.

Day 64

Wednesday, 20 May

I was musing yesterday about the inequality of our world's water supply. Some have more than enough and can often afford to waste it, whilst others have too little. The same goes for food, so on this third Rogation Day I'm praying for a fairer sharing of the world's food resources. Which, surprisingly, leads me on to the Silton vestry mouse. Attracted immediately to some peanut butter, she has now been safely rehomed. Efforts are now underway to catch her friend, the bell tower mouse, who seems to have taken a liking to the bell ringers' peppermints. Now that's food sharing!

Day 65

Thursday, 21 May – Ascension Day

I'll be in church again today as it's one of the twelve Principal Holy Days in the Christian Year. (Quick Quiz: name them!) I do appreciate how fortunate I am to be amongst those allowed to enter our churches alone at the moment, and I know how you yearn to be able to do the same. I pray that the day is near when our churches will be open to you all for private prayer, meditation, silence, and peace. Today we remember when Jesus returned to his Father and made way for the coming of the Holy Spirit. His bodily presence was no longer necessary for his followers, but he promises to be spiritually present with us for ever: "Remember, I am with you always, to the end of the age."

Day 66

Friday, 22 May

With Jesus now enthroned in the heavenly realms, we must pray for the Church that he left to continue his work on earth. *Thy Kingdom Come* is a global prayer movement that invites us to join with other Christians around the world praying, in these nine days between Ascension and Pentecost, for more people to come to know Jesus. Every Christian is a kingdom builder. The more of us there are, proclaiming and practising Christ's saving love, the nearer the kingdom comes. Father, thy kingdom come; thy will be done; on earth as it is in heaven.

Day 67

Saturday, 23 May

Three pheasants have been daily visitors to our garden this spring, a cock and two hens. Survivors, maybe, from a nearby shoot, refugees from a war zone who've found sanctuary, food and water. Signs of the kingdom. I wondered at first if they were husband, wife and concubine – perhaps permissible in pheasant society. But I prefer to imagine them now as husband, wife and widowed sister, taken in to be cared for. It made me think how we should never make assumptions about others when we don't know their story. We shouldn't ever judge (Matthew 7:1). It just makes for a better world.

Day 68

Sunday, 24 May – Seventh Sunday of Easter

In Jesus's great prayer to his Father, he says: "I am not praying for the world, but for those you have given me... I will remain in the world no longer, but they are still in the world" (John 17:9,11). Our prayers for the Church that Christ left to continue his work on earth must surely include that she be committed to the needs of the world but never conformed to the world. We who are "still in the world" must seek continually to make it better, not adapt ourselves to fit into the world as it is. I can think of a lot we can do right now, calling out what is amiss in the world and rejoicing in signs of the kingdom.

Day 69

Monday, 25 May

I saw a Holly Blue in the meadow behind the house on our walk this morning – easy to identify, the only blue butterfly you're ever likely to see in all of Europe. A beautiful thing, a sign of the kingdom. Its caterpillars feed on the flowers and fruits of holly and ivy, which I suppose is why it's called a Holly Blue. We've got a holly tree in the back garden, so we're lucky. Holly and ivy. The Passion of Christ and everlasting life. Just made me think of Christmas. Will life be back to normal by then do you think? Will our Christmas services be just as they were last Christmas?

Day 70

Tuesday, 26 May

It was reported last week that global daily emissions of carbon dioxide in early April were down 17 per cent on average compared to 2019 levels. In the UK, the drop was a staggering 31 per cent. This is the "green lining" or "green dividend" of coronavirus. There is evidence already that more lives have been saved in China by cleaner air than were lost to Covid-19. The call now is for a "Reset", the necessity for these levels to be maintained after the pandemic has passed. It will mean making personal sacrifices, it will mean going without, it will mean doing things differently. Just how far are we prepared to go with that?

Day 71

Wednesday, 27 May

If life under lockdown is the template for a 31 per cent drop in UK carbon emissions, then we know what to do in the future: travel less. Before we even need to think about things like switching our home heating from gas/oil to electric, or buying an EV, we can just travel less – by plane and car, business and leisure – social, domestic and pleasure. It won't be pain free. The Revd Rachel Mash, Coordinator of Green Anglicans (can you be Anglican and not Green?), who is from the Anglican Church of Southern Africa, puts it like this: "Our current way of living is unsustainable, we are sick because the Earth is sick. We cannot go back to normal."

Day 72

Thursday, 28 May

An online poll of 2,053 people in Britain last week asked: "What are you most looking forward to when lockdown ends?" The top answer was Seeing friends and relatives, followed by Going to the hairdresser, Going on holiday, Going to the pub, Eating out, and Shopping. Next came Going to church. I was rather encouraged by that, particularly as church came ahead of sporting events and cinema. The spiritual life of our country is perhaps not in such bad shape as some people make it out to be, and I'm prepared to stick my neck out and say it's high time the government lifted the closure of our churches.

Day 73

Friday, 29 May

Canon Peter tipped me off that today is Oak Apple Day. I'm afraid I'd never heard of it and had to look it up, but you might be wearing a sprig of oak leaves. It commemorates the restoration of the English monarchy in 1660. The oak motif clearly relates to how Charles II once hid in an oak tree to escape the Roundheads, though it has nothing at all do with apples as we know them – an "oak apple", I learned, is a parasitic growth commonly found on oak trees. I like the idea. Our present Queen is not only a credit to our country but also Defender of the Faith and Supreme Governor of the Church of England. We should give thanks to God for her today.

Day 74

Saturday, 30 May

The Creator has scattered emeralds all over the garden. These sparkling green jewels, precious to God, are Mint Leaf Beetles. We counted seven this morning, glittering in the early sunlight. They feed on the mint but leave hardly any sign of damage. Mint is a vigorous plant and there's more than enough for all of us. These beautiful creatures have evolved for a purpose known only to God; all I know is they share this garden with us and have every bit as much right to be here as we do.

Day 75

Sunday, 31 May – Pentecost or Whitsunday

For St John there is no violent wind, tongues of fire and babel of voices as there are for St Luke. Only Christ's gentle breath and peace. No power from on high save the authority to forgive sins. But what a combo. Peace and forgiveness. Peace and forgiveness. If you were to walk the earth with a gospel of salvation for all the world, just as those first Spirit-filled followers of Christ did, what better news could you proclaim than that? Come Holy Spirit.

Day 76

Monday, 1 June – Visit of the Blessed Virgin Mary to Elizabeth (Transferred from yesterday)

The visit of the pregnant Mary to her pregnant cousin Elizabeth becomes the occasion for Mary to sing her great canticle of praise in honour of her Lord and God – the Magnificat. Mary's confession of God as "my Saviour" is our assertion too. God is our Saviour. It means we should look to no other power for salvation from the chaos we have created for ourselves. Neither scientific nor social progress; technology, education, legislation; none of these things can of themselves deliver us from the mess and madness of our world. God may use these things as God wills, but the basis of our trust, hope and commitment must, like Mary's, be clear: God is our Saviour.

Day 77

Tuesday, 2 June

The sunniest spring on record means my vegetables in the back garden have needed a bit of watering. But some years ago now I stopped watering the front (flower) garden. The main consequence is that the lawn goes brown. So I no longer mow it obsessively and leave a large circle in the middle uncut. It's now full of meadow buttercups, meadow vetchling, birdsfoot trefoil, knapweed, scabious and many other native species beloved by bees, bugs and butterflies. One of the great delights at this time of year is watching the goldfinches descending on it to eat the seed heads of the hawksbeard. I counted eight in one flock this morning. Pure joy. Eve wants us all to go wild this month (#30DaysWild) – I recommend it!

Day 78

Wednesday, 3 June

A parishioner – we'll call him John because that is in fact his name – wrote to tell me about his small garden pond in the middle of the town. It had become totally overgrown, more vegetation than water. He spent days clearing it out until all that remained was a damaged liner that needed to be replaced – a job that had to wait. Before he got round to doing it, he went out one day earlier this year and saw in a tiny pool of rainwater that had collected at the bottom... frog spawn! The value of the pond immediately became apparent. So he recovered the frog spawn, put in a new liner, and today those tadpoles are becoming frogs. There are water boatmen, dragonflies, and the birds drink and bathe in it. John knows it's the water of life.

Day 79

Thursday, 4 June

You can visit a car showroom today but you can't get christened. (According to the C of E website, only emergency baptisms at home or in hospital are allowed, "subject to strict hygiene precautions and physical distancing as far as this is possible.") I can't help feeling there's something wrong here. Isn't faith just being relegated to a matter of zero importance – at least not as important as buying a new car? There could easily be a christening in the churchyard today: candidate, parents, two godparents plus me = six. I plan to use a tin mug tied to the end of a two-metre stick, or even a water pistol. We just have to start thinking outside the box.

Day 80

Friday, 5 June

You can get a pizza from a takeaway restaurant but you can't get holy communion. In other words, you can get bread with cheese and tomatoes on it but you can't get the bread of life. In a dream I'm dressed in PPE distributing wafers, properly and reverently consecrated, from the church porch. The faithful are filing past, two metres apart. (Or perhaps we could operate a drive-through from the end of the church path.) Afterwards, the LPAs take it to those who can't get out. Quite seriously, if Deliveroo can do it, why can't we? Extraordinary times call for extraordinary measures. If our heavenly food were regarded by the rule makers to be as important as our earthly food, it wouldn't just be a dream. It would be happening.

Day 81

Saturday, 6 June

A leading immunologist in the US, Dr Andrew Fauci, has said, "I don't think we should ever shake hands again." It sounds dramatic, but it would obviously do a lot to slow the spread of all germs and viruses. But what do we do when we get back into church, at the door and during the Peace? Perhaps the Japanese *yumi*, a deep bow with hands pressed against the sides. Or the Thai *wai*, a slight bow with palms pressed together in a prayer-like fashion. Or perhaps the Hindu *namaste*, the spoken greeting accompanied by a similar hand gesture to the *wai*. It means something like, "the divine in me greets the divine in you". I like that. Eminently suitable for Christ-bearers like us.

Day 82

Sunday, 7 June – Trinity Sunday

It's wonderful to hear the news today that places of worship will be permitted to reopen on 15 June for individual prayer in line with social distancing guidelines, a date previously set as 4 July earliest. Although no communal worship will be allowed, it's a great sign of hope for the future. We must of course wait to see how this plays out at a local level and ensure that the hygiene and safety instructions that we will be given are carefully observed. It's good to be three parishes and churches together this Trinity Sunday, united in our love of God who is Father, Son and Holy Spirit. Like the characters in Leo Tolstoy's story *The Three Hermits*, together we can pray to God: "Three are thee and three are we, have mercy on us."

Day 83

Monday, 8 June

Do you think that God was the author of Covid-19 and has used it to call us to self-examination and repentance? A letter to the FT (a far more multifaceted newspaper than many people think) says, "Epidemics, wars and famines are God's ways of chastising whole peoples... As a society [we] are being called to measure ourselves against divine law and correct our failings." I can understand the point that God is the Creator of viruses (as of all else) and that good things ought to come from this. But for this virus to jump to humans from live chickens being butchered in a wet market in Wuhan can never have been God's intention. It would be like saying God created the hydrogen bomb. No, this virus is an evil killer, and there is no evil in the heart of God.

Day 84

Tuesday, 9 June

The meadows around here for the past few days have been alive with Meadow Brown butterflies, scores of them playing over the long grass and feeding on the nectar of the wildflowers. Butterflies and viruses, beauty and ugliness, tenderness and cruelty, order and chaos. Nature's many voices seem to contradict one another. It's hard to see God in a cobra or a volcano. Butterflies and summer skies tell of a God of beauty and love, but plagues and earthquakes cry out against that message. Perhaps they are just God's cross. And we know that the cross is followed by an empty tomb and victory.

Day 85

Wednesday, 10 June

Some people are speculating about how this pandemic might change the world; nearly everyone is agreed that progressive change must come from it. And everything is up for grabs. Not only green initiatives but also social change: action on poverty, civil rights and racial justice. So many inequalities have been heightened. Trouble is, we're living in an age of nationalism. Each country will take its own path. (Oddly, the US has already distanced itself from the WHO.) And I think that's a shame, because not only is international cooperation the best way for any real and lasting change to come about, but also every person in the world is our brother and sister, children of the same heavenly Father.

Day 86

Thursday, 11 June – Corpus Christi

This Thursday after Trinity Sunday is always kept as the Day of Thanksgiving for Holy Communion, which as we know was instituted on a Thursday (during the Last Supper). Every celebration of Holy Communion is a thanksgiving to God, recalling the price of our redemption and the source of our life. But today we have the opportunity to thank God for our spiritual food and drink itself. Sublime in its simplicity, the Sacrament is Christ and Christ is God, the means by which God comes to dwell in us and we in him, making us one with Christ and strengthening us in his service. And oh how we hunger and thirst for it now!

Day 87

Friday, 12 June – St Barnabas, Apostle
(Transferred from yesterday)

Not one of the Twelve but an early member of the Jerusalem church who was sent to Antioch where he became a co-worker and companion of St Paul and a key figure in the gentile mission. I don't know why but his popular symbol is the rose. In days of old his feast day was celebrated by the wearing of roses, which of course are in full bloom across much of Christendom. What's your favourite rose? To celebrate St Barnabas, send me a photo of it – taken in your garden please not from Google Images – together with its name, by midnight on Sunday, and I'll choose a winner to put on the church website.

Day 88

Saturday, 13 June

Yet another casualty of Covid-19 is today's Queen's Birthday Parade, cancelled for only the second time in her 68-year reign. (I know you'll be wondering – the national rail strike of 1955.) At the same time, thousands of people are expected to gather in central London for a demonstration in support of Black Lives Matter. The Cenotaph and a statue of Sir Winston Churchill have been boarded up. What if the two marches had clashed? We're living in extraordinary times. Happily, the Colour of the Welsh Guards will still be Trooped in a small and brief ceremony inside Windsor Castle. Happy birthday, ma'am. God save the Queen.

Day 89

Sunday, 14 June – First Sunday after Trinity

Churchill was a key figure in the defeat of German National Socialism. But yesterday, self-styled protectors of his statue appeared to be giving the Nazi salute. The world's gone mad. Violence spreads like a virus. We're dancing with the devil. And in today's gospel, the Mission of the Twelve, Jesus says, "See, I am sending you out like sheep into the midst of wolves." As his instructions unfold, it becomes crystal clear that in a dangerous world, in the face of persecution and suffering, the Christian way is one of non-confrontation and non-resistance to violence. May we be faithful followers in the way that Christ taught.

Day 90

Monday, 15 June

My Inbox is bulging with photos of gorgeous roses. Beauty for brokenness. A big thank you to everyone who sent one in and I'm sorry if you didn't get an individual reply – I was somewhat overwhelmed. In a totally arbitrary fashion I judge the winner to be Janet Botterill for this stunning picture of Lady of Shalott. (My David Austin Handbook of Roses tells me the name is the title of a poem by Tennyson and it was bred to commemorate the 200th anniversary of his birth in 1809.) Perhaps we might also remember that besides St Barnabas the rose is also a symbol of our very own St Mary, the Mystic Rose. Red for her love and white for her purity, she is rightly represented by the most beautiful of all flowers.

Day 91

Tuesday, 16 June

Last Friday we took the cat to the vet for her annual health check and booster jabs. Having been told to knock on the door and wait outside, we were greeted by the vet in full PPE – face mask, visor, apron and gloves. Pets, we're told, can pass on the virus. The instant I saw her (the vet, that is) I was reminded of the passage in Ephesians about the "whole armour of God": the belt of truth, the breastplate of righteousness, the shoes of peace, the shield of faith, the helmet of salvation and the sword of the Spirit. What protection we have! "Be strong in the Lord and in the strength of his power" (Ephesians 6:10).

Day 92

Wednesday, 17 June

Some years ago I went into Milton Primary School and the children were already gathered in the hall for assembly. They were chanting, One-world-think-glo-bal, One-world-think-glo-bal, over and over again. I remember at the time thinking what a wonderful mantra it was for children to be reciting, and how great it would be if we grownups could do the same. With all the racism, xenophobia and religious hatred going on in the world, fuelled by isolationism and a toxic nationalism, I can just hear it beating in my ears once again, One-world-think-glo-bal, One-world-think-glo-bal. Because all are one in Christ.

Day 93

Thursday, 18 June

At 11:20am on this day in 1944, a V1 flying bomb hit the Guards' Chapel on Birdcage Walk in London. It was a Sunday morning, worship was in progress, and 121 people were killed. Hitler didn't manage to close our churches but coronavirus has. News this week that 235 Covid-19 cases have been linked to a church in Oregon proves it was the right thing to do. Apparently this particular church continued having services in April and May, including a wedding for more than a hundred people! We must now be patient and make plans to reopen our churches safely. Our three PCCs are working on that at the moment and we should pray for them as they act on our behalf.

Day 94

Friday, 19 June

I don't know about you but I've never taken part in a lockdown quiz or happy hour. Zoom fatigue set in quite early for me, but then I do have Arabella and it must be quite different if you're living on your own. Twice I've had a group video call with friends, but just like online church meetings I've never really got used to people talking over each other and the distraction of seeing my own face when speaking. It only goes to prove that real life, in-the-flesh, face-to-face interactions are the ones humans are best at. They build trust and empathy. I bet we'll look back on lockdown as the time we really learnt that.

Day 95

Saturday, 20 June

I'm not a Druid or anything but I've always been rather enthralled by the longest day. I've also learnt over the years never to be travelling eastbound on the A303. "God called the light Day, and the darkness he called Night" – Genesis 1:5. This particular day that God in his great goodness has given us will last for seventeen hours, sunrise to sunset. I happened to be awake at four-thirty this morning and it was already light. I went back to sleep. It'll probably still be light when I go up to bed. What a day! Enjoy as much of it as you can.

Day 96

Sunday, 21 June – Second Sunday after Trinity
(And Father's Day)

For a couple of weeks we saw only the cock pheasant, never the two hens. That is until just the other day when Arabella went out the front door and spotted one of them… along with her chicks! So happy Father's Day, Fez, and to all of you who are being feted today. Others will be celebrating with their fathers today, or simply remembering those upon another shore and in a greater light. And we can all give thanks today for our Father in heaven, who "by his great mercy has given us a new birth into a living hope through the resurrection of Jesus Christ from the dead" (1 Peter 1:3).

Day 97

Monday, 22 June

I recently discovered a website that tells you all the so-called "awareness" days and weeks that fill the year. Today is the start of National Picnic Week, Breathe Easy Week and World Wellbeing Week. It's also Children's Hospice Week, and Anne Kings in Gillingham is doing a wonderful thing to raise money for Julia's House in Corfe Mullen. Anne has written a children's story called *Button Cottage Lockdown*. I've read it and I think it's really good. She'd like to give you a copy in exchange for a donation to Julia's House, which is a really great idea. Please contact her if you'd like to help raise some money for Julia's House this Children's Hospice Week.

Day 98

Tuesday, 23 June

They say we're about to get the hottest weather of the year so far. The swallows were out early this morning, riding the high currents, mouths open like nets to catch their insect breakfast. They're amazing creatures these summer visitors to our shores, who have come all the way from South Africa and Namibia. A journey of six thousand miles, covered at the rate of two hundred a day. They've crossed the Congo rainforest, the Sahara desert, Morocco, Spain and France. One world, think global.

Day 99

Wednesday, 24 June – Birth of John the Baptist

It's tremendous news that public worship can – but locally might not – resume on 4 July, with restrictions. It means you won't have to go on enduring these daily thoughts! It will be a relief for me, too, I assure you, though it has been fun. One of the things I've tried to do along the way is to keep us in time with the rhythm of the Christian year, and today the Church marks the birth of John the Baptist. John was endowed with God's grace even in the womb, and was born to lead us in repentance and to know Christ's forgiveness and life-giving love.

Born six months before Jesus, he was Christ's forerunner in life as well as in death.

Day 100

Thursday, 25 June

I started these thoughts on 18 March, the day after the C of E announced it would suspend public worship to slow the spread of coronavirus. It was a Wednesday and I was meant to be presiding at the mid-week Eucharist at St Mary's... the first service that didn't happen. That was a long time ago now, a hundred days to be precise. Quite a few of you have already told me you won't be going back to church any time soon, the risks being still too great, so could I please go on doing this? Well, sadly no, Saturday 4 July will be the last. And then it won't be long, I hope, before we meet for real. "For now we see in a mirror, dimly, but then we will see face to face" (1 Corinthians 13:12).

Day 101

Friday, 26 June

The easing of lockdown on 4 July could, of course, be only temporary. If things take a turn for the worse a stricter regime like we're in now would be reintroduced. I've heard it said that some measures may remain in place even until next spring. It made me wonder how long it took for life to get back to normal after the outbreak of Spanish flu in 1918, which killed an estimated forty million people worldwide. In Britain, where wartime hardship and malnutrition had weakened the population's resistance to the pandemic, 250,000 died. The fear must have been far greater even than it is now. But you know what? The time came when people started hugging again.

Day 102

Saturday, 27 June

Pictures of the tons of rubbish left behind on Bournemouth Beach left me stunned. Have so many people already forgotten David Attenborough's heart-rending images of marine life caught up in floating plastic? I was already worried that coronavirus had taken the impetus out of the War on Plastic, which at the start of the year had seemed to be gathering momentum. Wet wipes and single use plastic are considered fair game once more in the name of health and safety, and that may be OK. But the scenes on the beaches? No, that's not OK. It makes me feel ashamed to be human. The planet needs healing, and the human race needs saving from its deplorable selfishness. Come, Lord Jesus.

Day 103

Sunday, 28 June – Third Sunday after Trinity

The Petertide ordination of priests and deacons – which unavoidably necessitates the laying-on of hands – has been postponed from this weekend until September. Instead, this afternoon, Bishop Nicholas will license thirteen deacons-to-be as lay workers on Zoom. Now isn't that a sign of the times? These new curates will become another feature in the strange history of 2020. As always we should pray for the ministries of these women and men who will be serving in Salisbury Diocese. Please remember them in your prayers today: Adrian, Ali, Caroline, Gerry, Helen, Helen, Karen, Katie, Leila, Matt, Nick, Nick and Sharon. May the Lord strengthen them in their work for his kingdom.

Day 104

Monday, 29 June – St Peter and St Paul, Apostles

Martyred together on this day in Rome in AD 64. Peter was nailed to a cross as a public spectacle at Nero's circus, upside down at his own request: he considered himself unworthy to die in the same way as his Lord, and also he wanted to face heavenward as he died. Paul was less-publicly executed, beheaded with a sword outside the city walls, his last prerogative as a Roman citizen. I believe there was a man called Jesus of Nazareth who God raised from the dead, not only because I read it in the Gospel but because Peter and Paul were prepared to die for that truth. I do not believe they would have been prepared to die for a lie.

Day 105

Tuesday, 30 June

Lockdown wasn't enough to heal the earth. Even though CO_2 emissions fell considerably for a couple of months, it was just a blip on a planetary scale. Last month was the hottest May globally ever recorded; ice is melting in Greenland at a rate never seen before; a team of polar scientists who had planned to leave by air had to leave by boat – there was no ice for their aeroplane to land on. Is there any hope? Yes. Coronavirus has prompted a shift in our values and attitudes: many have prioritized collective safety over individual freedom; distant threats are considered worth preparing for. Over an extended period of reflection we've had a chance to reimagine our future.

Day 106

Wednesday, 1 July

Whilst the human race has been preoccupied with coronavirus there have been constant reminders that the world is much bigger than us. The sun has risen every morning, bang on cue. Spring has given way to summer. The tadpoles have hatched, turned into frogs, and climbed out of the pond. The pheasant has had chicks. The broad beans I sowed on 1st March are plants four feet high and bearing gifts. Pages of the calendar have been torn away by time, and the world just keeps on turning.

Day 107

Thursday, 2 July

The hollyhocks are starting to flower, whose name derives from "holy hock". One story is that it was brought back from the Holy Land by the crusaders, another that it grew on Holy Island near St Cuthbert's hermit cell and became holy by his proximity. And in my mini meadow the lady's bedstraw is covered in whorls of bright yellow flowers. The story goes that the manger in the stable at Bethlehem was empty because the animals had eaten all the hay, so Mary laid the baby Jesus on a bed of this beautiful sprawling perennial - lady's bedstraw. All of the natural world is God's handiwork. How right and proper that so much of it tells the Christian story.

Day 108

Friday, 3 July – St Thomas, Apostle

Usually remembered in one word, "Doubting", an unfair epithet for a man who only asked for some proof. In fact the evidence he demanded was no more than what the other disciples had already been given the time that Thomas wasn't with them. I'd rather remember him as the one who, responding to Christ's command to "make disciples of all nations", went to India, where he built a church with his own hands. Celebrated as the patron saint of builders, his symbol consists of a carpenter's square… along with a spear, the instrument of his martyrdom.

Day 109

Saturday, 4 July

Fittingly, perhaps, Independence Day, the Fourth of July, the day we go forward as we each see fit, some to church and others not yet, but bound together in love with cords that cannot be broken.

We are the family of God,
we are his promise divine,
we are his chosen desire,
we are the glorious new wine.

(Bob Gillman, *Bind us together, Lord*)

Printed in Great Britain
by Amazon